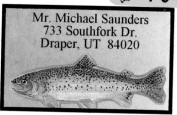

Mr. Michael Saunders
733 Southfork Dr.
Draper, UT 84020

LIVEBEARING AQUARIUM FISHES

BY MANFRED BREMBACH

Photography

DR. HERBERT R. AXELROD: 41 top, 50 top; 67 top, 69 top, 70 bottom, 76 top, 85 top, 123 bottom; MANFRED BREMBACH: 25, 29 bottom, 53 top, 65 top, 93 top, 103 top, 117 top, 121; RUTH BREWER: 103 bottom; J. ELIAS: 53 bottom, 95 bottom; DR. S. FRANK: 13 bottom; DAN FROMM: 59 bottom; MICHAEL GILROY: 40, 42; DR. HARRY GRIER: 1; H. HANSEN: 87 top, 127 bottom; B. KAHL: 5 top, 47 bottom, 65 bottom, 73, 87 bottom, 119 bottom; H. KYSELOV: 5 bottom, 39 bottom; C.O. MASTERS: 19 bottom; MANFRED MEYER: 55 top, 58, 81 top; AARON NORMAN: 112; DR. JOANNE NORTON: 74; H.J. RICHTER: 15 bottom, 23, 29 top, 31, 57, 59 top, 71 bottom, 75 top and center, 83 bottom, 89, 95 top, 99, 101, 105, 107, 109, 111, 113, 115, 117 bottom; A. ROTH: 37, 61 top, 50 bottom, 51 top, 71 middle, 75 bottom, 123 top, 125 top, 127 top; GLEN Y. TAKESHITA: 76 bottom; MITSUYOSHI TATEMATSU, courtesy *Midori Shobo*, Fish Magazine, Japan: 13; EDWARD C. TAYLOR: 97 top; DR. ANTHONY TERCEIRA: 97 bottom; 19 top right, 125 bottom; A. VAN DEN NIEUWENHUIZEN: 79, 119 top; DR. C. D. ZANDER: 81 bottom; R. ZUKAL: 15 top, 27 top, 33 bottom, 45 bottom, 47 top, 49, 55 bottom, 71 bottom, 83 top, 85 top, 91, 93 bottom.

TRANSLATED BY CHRISTA AHRENS

ISBN 0-86622-101-8

Originally published in German by Franckh'sche Verlagshandlung, W. Keller & Co., Stuttgart 1979 under the title *Lebendgebarende Fische im Aquarium*. First edition © 1979 by Franckh'sche Verlagshandlung.

Distributed in the UNITED STATES by T.F.H. Publications, Inc., 211 West Sylvania Avenue, Neptune City, NJ 07753; in CANADA by H & L Pet Supplies Inc., 27 Kingston Crescent, Kitchener, Ontario N2B 2T6; Rolf C. Hagen Ltd., 3225 Sartelon Street, Montreal 382 Quebec; in ENGLAND by T.F.H. Publications Limited, 4 Kier Park, Ascot, Berkshire SL5 7DS; in AUSTRALIA AND THE SOUTH PACIFIC by T.F.H. (Australia) Pty. Ltd., Box 149, Brookvale 2100 N.S.W., Australia; in NEW ZEALAND by Ross Haines & Son, Ltd., 18 Monmouth Street, Grey Lynn, Auckland 2 New Zealand; in SINGAPORE AND MALAYSIA by MPH Distributors (S) Pte., Ltd., 601 Sims Drive, # 03/07/21, Singapore 1438; in the PHILIPPINES by Bio-Research, 5 Lippay Street, San Lorenzo Village, Makati Rizal; in SOUTH AFRICA by Multipet Pty. Ltd., 30 Turners Avenue, Durban 4001. Published by T.F.H. Publications Inc. Manufactured in the United States of America by T.F.H. Publications, Inc.

Contents

What Are Livebearers?

The term "livebearers" is applied to various groups of fishes not all of which are related to one another. Hence the livebearers do not form a special taxonomic unit but rather should be understood as a collective term. Many marine sharks give birth to living young. Thus the offspring of the white shark, for example, may measure as much as 4½ feet at the time of its birth. The Norway haddock occurs in the northern Atlantic and is familiar to many hobbyists as a food fish. But how many people realize that this fish, too, is a "livebearer"? And what a livebearer! One female may produce 300,000 larvae at a time! There is even a livebearer native to temperate Europe. This is the viviparous blenny, a fish which, although called "eel mother" in German, is neither the "mother of the eel" nor related to the latter. But the species is nonetheless a livebearer and can be caught off the Baltic coast. These and many other marine fishes, which can be kept in aquaria only with difficulty, will be given only a passing mention as livebearers here, without being referred to in greater detail. But there are a whole range of small and minute livebearing freshwater fishes which do not require a large tank and are fairly easy to keep. These will be discussed in this book.

Viviparity (giving birth to living young) occurs in the following freshwater aquarium fish families:

1. Poeciliidae—Poeciliids, Typical Livebearers
2. Goodeidae—Goodeids
3. Hemiramphidae—halfbeaks
4. Jenynsiidae—One-sided Livebearers
5. Anablepidae—Foureyes

According to an accepted modern classification, all these families belong to a single order, the Atheriniformes. With the exception of the Anablepidae, which are likely to con-

The guppy (two males shown above, female shown below) is generally agreed upon as being the most commonly kept of the livebearing fish species in freshwater aquaria, but other species in the family Poeciliidae rival it—and at times even exceed it—in popularity.

tinue to be maintained primarily in large show tanks, representatives of all these families are now being kept and bred in home aquaria. However, despite their growing importance in the aquarium hobby, the livebearers form only a very small proportion of the known fish species. Of the 300 families of Teleostei (bony fishes) known today, fewer than 10 families can be described as livebearers. The percentage is even smaller when it comes to number of species: the livebearers make up a mere 1% of all known species.

Keeping Livebearers

Experience has shown that the livebearers discussed in this book can be kept and bred in ordinary tap-water of medium hardness (10 to 20 DH.). For this reason the Poeciliidae in particular have gained the reputation of being "hardy" aquarium fishes suitable for beginners. Instead of discussing the "hardy" livebearers, it would be more accurate to use the description "well-established aquarium strains," for only these have proven to be relatively resistant and robust. On the other hand, if one brings back wild specimens and transfers them straight from their native water into the aquarium, then there will be no end of trouble. It was only through the process of domestication, breeding the fish in home aquaria over many generations, that previously difficult species have evolved into undemanding pets! I shall here be discussing primarily those livebearers which show promise for development into good aquarium fishes or have already become so. Extremely soft water should never be used for livebearers. Where nothing but soft tap-water is available one has to increase its hardness.

While normally making only modest demands where water hardness is concerned, the majority of livebearers tend to

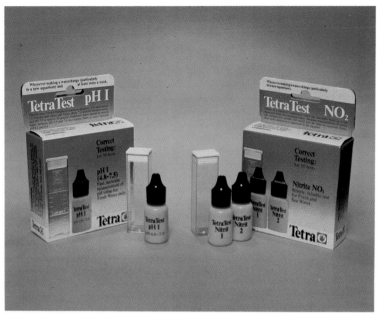

Test kits that allow the aquarist to check the pH, hardness and nitrite/nitrate content of the aquarium water are valuable tools in helping to provide optimum water conditions for livebearers.

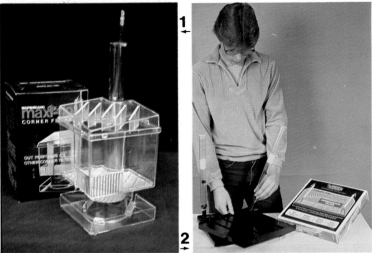

Various types of filtering devices currently on the maket. Below are shown an inside corner filter, outside power filter and sponge filters; above and on facing page are shown 1. inside corner filter with airstone to boost efficiency; 2. undergravel filter; 3. outside hanging power filter; 4. canister power filter; 5. diatomaceous earth power filter.

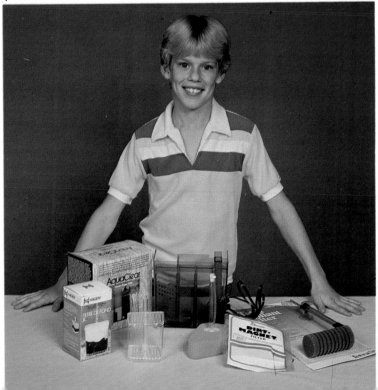

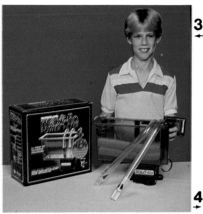

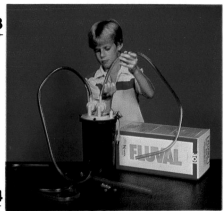

react very strongly in another respect. Since many species occur naturally in running water with a high oxygen content, they demand water of great purity which contains no nitrogenous waste-products such as ammonia, nitrite, and nitrate.

The neglect of this single point is responsible for many failures following what at first were apparently successful breeding ventures. In a heavily stocked community tank one should thus check regularly on these values with one of the water chemistry test kits sold for this purpose. The chemical tests are generally unnecessary where ¼ to ⅓ of the aquarium water is replaced with new water at weekly intervals. The wastes of the fishes are removed as reliably by this simple procedure as are food left-overs.

The livebearer aquarium should be equipped at all times with efficient internal filters (especially in small tanks) or with adequate external filters (most appropriate with larger tanks). The filter element should be cleaned with cold water at frequent intervals but should not be boiled as this would destroy important bacterial cultures.

Livebearers tolerate pH values within the range of 7 to 8, thus again not making any special demands on the hobbyist. Temperature requirements are included in the descriptions of each species. Where suggested partial water changes are made each week, the tap-water can usually be poured straight into the aquarium provided it has the correct degree of hardness. Otherwise the water must be prepared and left to stand for a day or two in a well-ventilated place, particularly if it contains chlorine.

Those species whose natural environment consists of brackish water (sailfin molly, *Poecilia latipinna*; one-sided livebearer; pike topminnow; and several *Dermogenys* species) can be kept in pure fresh water in community situations after gradual acclimation. A mixed population comprising representatives of the various livebearing families, such as Poeciliidae and Goodeidae species as well as a few of the halfbeaks, in a larger aquarium can be very attractive. If you investigate

Sponge filters (right) are especially useful in tanks containing livebearer fry.

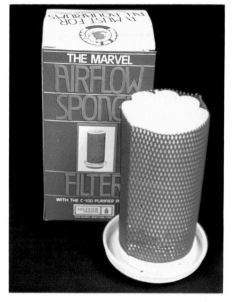

Below: dependable heaters and airpumps can be vital pieces of equipment.

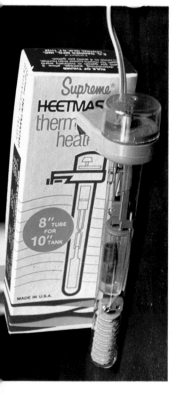

beforehand the living requirements and behavior of the various species, you can assemble an aquarium collection that will always provide interest and instruction.

The aquarist should not mix species which have a tendency toward hybridization, such as those of the genera *Xiphophorus* and *Poecilia* (from the *Limia* and *Mollienesia* groups), or that have the same requirements as far as habitat and food are concerned, such as the various halfbeak species. In the confined space of the aquarium the dominant species would inevitably bully the smaller one and prevent it from getting adequate food. If you do intend to set up a community tank, remember the most important principle: soft and acid water is suitable for many species of fishes, but definitely not for livebearers.

Breeding Livebearing Aquarium Fishes

Among the livebearers there are species that can be bred with very little effort. But propagation does not necessarily mean cultivation. Many of the platies, swordtails, and mollies available on the market today are the result of painstakingly hard work and genetically convoluted selective breeding. This type of highly specialized selective breeding is not always essential. It is a business that apart from a great deal of practical experience, genetic knowledge, and a considerable investment in aquariums also requires an "instinct" and a good bit of luck. However, if you happen to have purchased a pair of breathtakingly beautiful swordtails or platies, remember that if you want to see the same attributes in their progeny you always need two homozygous, or genetically identical, individuals, and often the female that would

Today's guppies are greatly different in appearance (and size) from wild guppies and the first domesticated strains. The finnage of both the male (above) and female guppy shown here are much more extensive and colorful than the finnage of wild-type guppies.

perfectly match that handsome male is thousands of miles away in Singapore. For the average aquarist, therefore, such selective breeding attempts often bear the label "to be used once only." However, anyone who is genuinely interested in selective breeding of aquarium fishes should consult the special literature and join the appropriate aquarium societies.

The selective breeding of livebearers serves one other purpose: the preservation and continued cultivation of pure aquarium strains. Every aquarist should approach any breeding attempt with this in mind. Each fish species that reaches our tanks through imports inevitably becomes subject to a process of selection which may eventually end with domestication. The guppy is perhaps the best example of this. Only those species which have managed to adapt to the new and essentially artificial demands of the aquarium world—these often in stark contrast to the demands of the natural environment—have become popular aquarium fishes. Many species are threatened with extinction in the wild state, and for this reason alone we must intelligently strive to ensure their propagation in captivity. What is important here is that wherever possible the natural coloration and modes of behavior should be retained in the domestic forms. Observant aquarists noted that some wild fishes, such as *Belonesox*, *Xiphophorus helleri*, and more recently *Priapella intermedia* and *Xenotoca eiseni*, developed into resistant aquarium strains only very gradually, after a consolidation process which frequently involved considerable losses. A large proportion of the fishes available today are the descendants of just a few parents that were of the minority that survived the stresses and strains of the enforced transfer from nature to the aquarium.

For breeding purposes the aquarist will require, along with the normal room aquarium, at least three smaller (10 to 15 gallons) tanks and several very small (about one to 3 gallons) tanks. The smallest tanks, equipped with an airstone and Java moss or other dense plants, serve as breeding tanks

Belonesox belizanus (pair shown above) and *Xenotoca eiseni* (below) are representative of species whose wild stock did not acclimate readily to aquarium life; it took a number of generations before a stable aquarium stock was developed.

in which gravid females give birth to their young. The young are later transferred to one of the larger tanks, which should be well seasoned. The breeding tanks should be filled with water taken from these. In the largest tanks the young are offered a good, nourishing diet of *Artemia* and fine powdered food until it becomes possible to sex them. Fishes selected for breeding purposes should complete their development in the remaining tanks, with males and females separated from each other. Why go to all this trouble? One characteristic of all Poeciliidae and halfbeaks is superfetation. For example, after a single fertilization a guppy or *Dermogenys* female can produce several broods of young without requiring contact with a male again during the intervals! The sperm is stored and nourished in the folds of the ovary and remains fertile for a period of up to several months. It is vital to bear this in mind if one wants to separate a female from a group of sexually mature fish and use her for breeding.

If necessary, the female should be kept separate from the males for one or two breeding periods (about two months) so it is certain she does not contain any unwanted sperm. On the other hand, it has been observed that it is always the most recently deposited sperm that is most viable in the fertilization of new eggs. This means that it likely will be the sperm from the last male to inseminate the female that fertilizes the eggs.

The Goodeidae make life considerably easier for the breeder in one respect: as far as is known, such a degree of superfetation does not occur in these fishes. Each time the female produces young, renewed fertilization is necessary.

Almost all Poeciliidae and Goodeidae, as well as a few halfbeaks (*Dermogenys*), become ready for fertilization at regular intervals. In other words, these fishes can produce young the year around and are not dependent on specific breeding seasons.

The length of the gestation period fluctuates in all livebearers within certain limits and is at least three weeks. It can, however, be extended by up to three times its normal

Commercially available breeding traps for livebearers can be useful devices, even though they are not equally suitable for use with all species. Shown here are a net-type trap and a compartmentized trap.

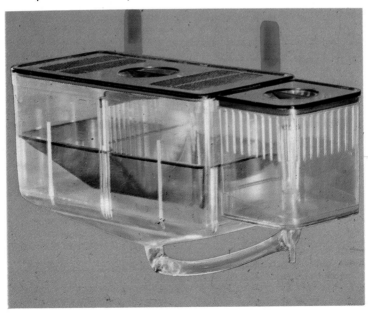

length and often terminated altogether by external factors such as temperature, poor diet, or harmful substances in the water. Many livebearers counteract such adversity with the astonishing ability to dissolve and then resorb their partially developed embryos.

Within the descriptions of the various species you will quite frequently encounter the term "hybrid." Hybrids are the progeny of two parent animals that belong to different species. In many cases the hybrids are nonviable to begin with. However, the livebearers include some species so closely related that their offspring *are* viable. I must add that the reproductive ability of such hybrids is either nonexistent or limited and physical malformations are frequent. If the aquarist is experienced and familiar with the science of genetics, planned hybridization can produce admirable results as demonstrated in the cultivation of the swordtail. Uncontrolled hybridization, such as may occur in a community tank between two closely related *Poecilia* species for example, leads to negative changes both externally and in the genetic make-up. This degeneration often results in the loss of precisely all those characteristics of a fish species the serious aquarist should endeavor to preserve!

Nutrition

Many livebearers are rightly described as omnivores. In their natural environment they frequently occur in the overgrown shore habitat where they find varied fare among the dense plant growth. Bearing in mind that many livebearers are surface feeders and in some cases devour insects in large quantities, some idea can be had as to what lies behind the requirement of "a varied diet." Even those species which are mainly vegetarian prey upon microorganisms (including tiny

Live foods are very good for the fish to eat—and it's fun to watch them eat them. Above, water fleas of the genus *Daphnia*; left, three types of insect larvae; below, adult brine shrimp.

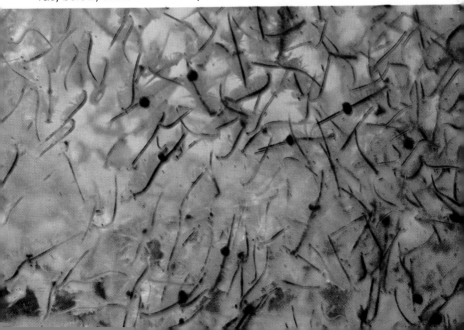

crustaceans and worms) as a supplement that should not be underestimated. The message to the aquarist is clear: under natural conditions the apparently undemanding "omnivores" avail themselves of a wide range of important animal as well as vegetable proteins, minerals, and vitamins. Hence successful breeding depends not only on water of the required purity and chemistry but also on correct nutrition. Most livebearers can be adapted to dried foods. I even managed this with the pike top minnow (*Belonesox*)! However, after a prolonged period of existing on nothing but dried foods a great many species begin to weaken and cease reproducing. On the other hand, dried food should by no means be scorned as a basic food. In the winter live foods are scarce, and for practical and financial reasons it is often not possible to provide live food on a daily basis.

Unless you happen to be keeping species with particularly demanding nutritional preferences, the following will serve as a guideline: apart from small amounts of dried food (never offer more than the fish can actually eat within 1 to 2 minutes!), daphnia or mosquito larvae should be supplied at least three times a week, varied with occasional feedings of tubifex. Fruitflies with stunted (vestigial) wings are an excellent breeding food for all fish species which also feed at the water's surface.

A collecting trip using a dipnet and bucket can not only be fun for the entire family but can also serve to vary the menu of your fish. Smaller flying insects captured in meadows and marshes ("meadow plankton") are equally as rich in vitamins as the mosquito larvae that can be found in spring and summer in the thousands in boggy ponds and other quiet bodies of water. Houseflies are a popular food with many livebearers, and avoid the necessity of administering synthetic vitamins, a practice that has become increasingly prevalent.

In this context I would also advocate the use of aquatic algae which for reasons of aquarium health and appearance are often despised. If an aquarium or its water is maintained

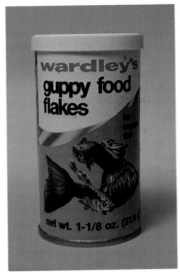

There is a great assortment of foods available, so it is easy for hobbyists to provide their fishes with a varied diet.

One of the most important factors in keeping livebearers is to make sure that the water in which they live is not loaded down with nitrogenous compounds resulting from the breakdown of organic materials, including the wastes produced by the fishes themselves, in the tank. Since filters will not remove such wastes completely, aquarists have to make frequent partial water changes in order to keep the water "fresh." Automatic water changers make sure that the job gets done reliably and without any effort on the hobbyist's part.

in the manner suggested, then good illumination and optimal fertilization (perhaps CO_2-fertilization) will not only result in a splendid ornamental plant growth but will encourage a modest bloom of green algae. Instead of cursing one's bad luck and reaching for the algicide tablets, one should learn to look at the microscopic plants with appreciation. Not only do they indicate that the aquarium is receiving the correct biological care, but they are among the best greenfoods livebearers can possibly get. The aquarist can, of course, boil lettuce leaves or use this as a medium for the cultivation of algae. Frozen spinach can be thawed and fed to the fish as well. I have achieved the best results by encouraging at least a moderate natural growth of algae in my tanks. Where the algae threaten to get out of control, the degree of growth can be minimized with the help of a few loaches, barbs, or plecostomus catfishes. Dried food with a vegetable base is successful as a fry food, and another particularly good source of nourishment is the nauplii of brine shrimp (*Artemia*). The small nauplii of *Cyclops* are acceptable fare, but the adult crustaceans can attack the gills of the fry. Fine foods in dry or liquid form can also be offered. Where halfbeaks are involved, springtails (collembola), which are often plentiful in older aquariums, make a good live food.

A useful though less esthetic supplement to the normal diet for adult fishes is their own young. The aquarist should avoid making any moral judgment concerning this particular peculiarity of the fish, which so often is described as "cannibalism" with certain immoral undertones. It is an essentially abnormal behavior which in fish is frequently caused by their enforced confinement in an aquarium. Possible reasons for cannibalism may be an overstocked tank with too much nitrate or too high a population density or a dietary deficiency.

Facing page:
A mother guppy chasing down a baby guppy; the different livebearer species vary in their inclination to eat their own young, but all livebearers are less likely to eat their young if they are well fed.

The Mechanics of Livebearing

An important prerequisite for viviparity is internal fertilization. The anal fin of the male has been transformed into an organ by means of which the transfer of the spermatozoa is effected. These copulatory organs are so distinct and characteristic in structure that they can serve to identify the different families.

The livebearers are so designed to effect the transfer of the spermatozoa in as compact a form as possible. For this reason most genera have evolved "sperm parcels" in which the spermatozoa are glued together with a gelatinous substance to form either a solid or a hollow ball. This ball does not dissolve and liberate the individual spermatozoa until it has reached the female's ovary. Research on swordtails has established that on average each sperm parcel of these fish is comprised of 5,500 spermatozoa.

Apart from producing the remarkable reproductive technique of transferring sperm parcels with the aid of specially adapted fins, Mother Nature had to muster a lot more invention in order to facilitate livebearing in fishes. From what we know about our own development inside the mother's body, we inevitably connect the livebearing process with such terms as "womb," "after-birth," or "umbilical cord." None of these anatomical features exist in fishes.

The livebearing fishes possess a single ovary as well as an oviduct which transports the eggs or embryos into the outside world. However, before we look at the alternatives that nature has devised to make up for the nonexistent uterus, let's sum up the basic problems of viviparity that need to be resolved.

Facing page:
Upper photo: closeup of gonopodium of male *Xiphophorus helleri*.
Lower photo: developing embryos of *Xiphophorus helleri*.

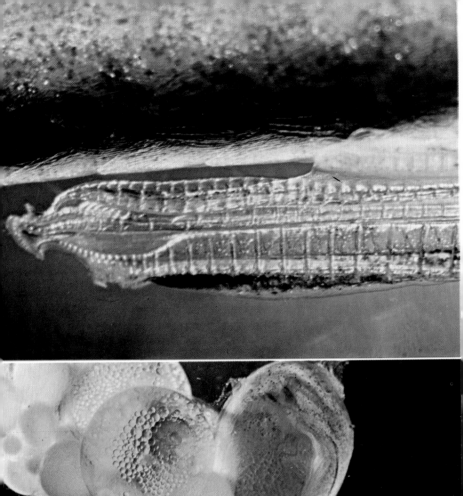

Cut off from the outside world, the growing embryos must be supplied with adequate nourishment and oxygen. In the same way, waste products and carbon dioxide must be removed from their environment. The livebearers have overcome these reproductive problems in a variety of ways.

The livebearing poeciliids, for example, have solved the foregoing problems in an astonishingly simple way. The fertilized eggs are not discharged straight into the water as they usually are in fishes but are retained in the ovary until the embryos have completed their development inside the egg. The eggs contain as much nutrient substance in the yolk as the embryos require for their full development. In early research, this type of livebearing was described as "ovoviviparity," which can be freely translated as "livebearing inside the egg-membrane." Some scientists speculated that once the eggs are fertilized they should also be able to develop outside the maternal ovary. They carried out the appropriate experiments and had to admit, when reviewing their inconclusive results, that ovoviviparity appeared not to consist of simple retention of the eggs after all. There must be processes of exchange—some of them still unknown—between embryo, egg membrane, and the maternal follicular cells surrounding the egg.

Eggs that are capable of undergoing fertilization must first be produced inside the ovary. The function of the follicular cells in this respect is to surround the initially very small egg-cell with yolk and with an egg membrane which completely encloses it. Over and above that they probably have a special part to play in supplying the embryos with oxygen.

But by what method do the developing fry assimilate oxygen at this early stage, before they possess functional gills?

These and other questions have been answered by the research work of C. L. Turner. Turner discovered the "neck strap" on the embryos of guppies, platies, swordtails, and other livebearers. The neck strap is an anatomical expansion of the yolk sac, wrapped over the embryo's head rather like a

There is no strict pattern of delivery among the livebearers as regards whether the fry are delivered head first or tail first or rolled up into a ball. The baby guppy above was delivered tail first, whereas the baby swordtail below is being delivered head first.

cap. A fine network of blood vessels surrounds both yolk sac and neck strap, transporting the nutrients of the yolk to the embryo. At the same time this network of blood vessels takes up the oxygen necessary for respiration which might be given off by the follicle cells. In accordance with this, the function of the "neck strap" is to likely make it easier for respiratory gases to be exchanged, and this would be achieved by a surface enlargement of both the yolk sac and the network of blood vessels.

As can be seen, even this—what is often described as a "simple" form of livebearing—betrays quite remarkable specialized adaptations when looked at in detail. The main characteristic of ovoviviparity is that the embryo always develops inside the egg membrane and without any recognizable forms of contact with the mother. The eggs are large, have a high yolk-content, and the egg membrane does not rupture until just prior to or immediately after birth. This can be seen very clearly in the birth of young guppies. Almost all livebearing poeciliids as well as the halfbeaks that have been discussed develop in accordance with this pattern.

Apart from ovoviviparity ("egg livebearing") there also exists a phenomenon that can be described as "true livebearing" or viviparity. The Goodeidae is an example. In this family the eggs are also fertilized inside the follicles, but after a short period of development they migrate into a saclike elastic expansion of the ovary. The eggs of the Goodeidae contain very little yolk and are consequently much smaller than the nutrient-rich eggs of the Poeciliidae. Hence the yolk supply in the Goodeidae lasts only for a few days and is then depleted. This is the point at which the embryos rupture the egg membranes and migrate into the elastic dilation of the ovary. The embryos now grow tube-like structures on the undersurfaces which, considering their function, can rightly be described as umbilical cords. The correct zoological term for them is *trophotaenia* ("feeding tapes"). The trophotaenia grow toward the wall of the ovary, make

The young of the goodeid species (a male of the goodeid species *Xenotoca eiseni* is shown in the upper photo) are born with tropho-taenia attached; the goodeid fry shown in the lower photo is *Xeno-toca eiseni*.

contact with it, and from there receive all the substances that are necessary for the development of the embryo. For one or two days after the young Goodeidae are born one can still see the trophotaenia on their abdomens. The tapes disappear only gradually and are a visible reminder of the varied paths along which nature has traveled during the evolution of the livebearing mode of reproduction.

While the umbilicus-like trophotaenia still lie well within the realm of human understanding, the path chosen by the one-sided livebearers defies all rational comparisons. The Jenynsiidae reproduce exactly the other way around: In this family the wall of the maternal ovary dispatches the feeding-tubes to the embryos, hooks them into the gill slits like bent fingers, and in this way supplies them with nourishment. It's not surprising that when the young one-sided livebearers are born their opercula are not yet fully developed and only gradually grow to their final size.

The genera *Heterandria* and *Poeciliopsis* should also be mentioned. Their embryonic development deviates from the usual ovoviviparity of the Poeciliidae. In some fishes of these genera the female develops structures which in certain respects can be compared to the placenta of mammals. These fishes are remarkable in another respect, too. In the least killifish *Heterandria formosa*, for example, the female does not produce all her young at once but within a specific period gives birth more or less in installments, delivering one to two young every day. The result is that the eggs are fertilized successively so that there are always several clutches of embryos of varying ages developing side by side.

The list of special adaptations made by our livebearers is a long one, and there is still a wealth of information left to report. However, it is beyond the scope of this book to more than briefly discuss the basics of livebearing fishes. It is hoped that what has been outlined in this chapter will be sufficient to spark an interest in further studies.

This young (but not newborn) *Xenotoca eiseni* still has trophotaenia attached.

Baby *Xenotoca eiseni* being delivered; in comparison with most poeciliid species, all of the goodeid species have relatively few fry at each delivery.

Behavior of Livebearers

The aquarist setting up an aquarium of livebearers will never be able to complain "there is nothing to look at." Courting and spawning go on all the time. Courtship and fighting between rivals become particularly intense and most fascinating to watch after one has isolated the male from the female for a few days. How intense courtship activity becomes depends much on the size of the aquarium. The courtship dance of the male swordtail, the way he elegantly darts back and forth, is exciting enough to watch if it takes place in a smaller tank, but in an aquarium with plenty of swimming space he can work himself up into a virtual frenzy. One begins to fear that at any moment he will come shooting out of the water at breakneck speed!

None the less fascinating are the bloodless fights between two halfbeak males with their beaks interlocked, or the ceaseless activity of a male blue limia, *Poecilia melanogaster*, in the community tank.

There is always "something going on" in an aquarium containing livebearers. It is important to record your observations and arrange them into categories according to similarities. The components of a behavioral sequence would all go together, for example, or they could be listed in the order of the frequency observed. Beware of jumping to conclusions or of generalizing from insufficient data! Modes of behavior can be intensified as in the wrestling halfbeak, or modified or negated by selective breeding.

I once kept several red swordtail males in association with one wild male. A few days later I introduced a female into the tank. The chaotic courting activity that ensued defies description. Within three minutes the wild swordtail male managed to drive the four red rivals away from the female, forced them all into one corner of the aquarium, courted the confused female at the same time, and made several attempts

With dorsal fin spread to its widest, this male sailfin molly impresses the female to which he is displaying as part of the courtship ritual.

The male *Heterandria formosa* actively pursues the much larger female during the mating procedure.

to copulate with her. The domestic swordtails were quite unable to hold their own when confronted with the wild male's passionate, assertive behavior! This is why one should always take the time to study very carefully the behavior of *any* animals one is thinking of using as breeders.

Family Poeciliidae— Typical livebearers

With about 150 known species, the Poeciliidae constitutes by far the largest family among the livebearers. In their original distribution they are confined largely to Central America, though representatives of the various genera can be found from the southeastern part of the United States through Mexico and Central America to as far south as Argentina and Peru. That one is today able to collect *Gambusia* in Yugoslavia and swordtails on Celebes is the direct result of experiments conducted in the use of the Poeciliidae in the control of mosquitoes. Another major factor in accidental distribution is that keeping aquarium fishes has become increasingly popular all over the world, with many specimens being released by accident or on purpose into the wilds.

The great majority of the Poeciliidae are small shallow-water fishes occurring in the overgrown shore habitats of streams, rivers, and ponds. Being surface feeders, they have vertical mouths with very fine teeth and the anterior part of the dorsal area is generally straight in profile. Sexual dimorphism, or the difference in appearance of males and females, is marked in some species. Common to all males is a copulatory organ called the gonopodium. This specialized organ is formed by the 3rd, 4th, and 5th rays of the anal fin and is a characteristic of this family. The gonopodium has complete-

Some of the livebearing species, especially those of the family Poeciliidae, have been introduced into waters to which they are not native as aids in the war against mosquitoes and other insect pests. The fishes shown here, for example, are North American poeciliids (top to bottom: swordtail pair, female *Gambusia affinis*, male *Gambusia affinis*) that were collected in the northern Australia/New Guinea area.

ly lost its function as an organ of locomotion but has an incredible range of movement. It can be moved in all directions, including forward. This is made possible by a special transformation of those skeletal parts that support the gonopodium and its muscles. Both this internal skeletal structure and the precise structure of the individual rays of the gonopodium are of the utmost importance in the assignment of taxonomic position to the various species and genera. In most genera the third and fourth anal fin rays bear fine structures at their tips called "hooks" and "claws." It has been found that these adaptations enable the males to actually hook their gonopodium into the female's genital pore. Normally the gonopodium is folded flat into a channel-like structure so that the rays lie parallel to each other. After a period of intense courtship the gonopodium is then hooked into position and the sperm parcels are deposited inside the ovary, in what can thus be considered genuine internal fertilization.

The detailed structure of the individual parts of the gonopodium may be of great taxonomic value to scientists but is apparently of little value to the fishes themselves. Males in which a severed gonopodium regenerated in a distorted manner continued to successfully inseminate females.

Artificial insemination by inserting sperm parcels into an anesthetized female with a fine pipette has been successfully carried out in the Poeciliidae. Because they are easy to breed and closely related species are capable of producing fertile hybrids, some species have become popular experimental fishes. Such research has provided science with answers to questions on genetics and behavior, notably aggression.

The Poeciliidae embraces more than 20 genera. With one exception, all species are livebearers.

Genus *Poecilia*

This large genus includes numerous species popular as aquarium fishes. Common to all species is a gonopodium which is less than one-third of the standard length of the

The ease of breeding many of the poeciliid species, coupled with the speed with which new generations can be produced, has caused the popular livebearers to be excellent subjects for experimentation in the development of new forms and colors. These high-finned and lyre-tailed black swordtails are the culmination of much planned breeding work, for example.

fish, measured from the tip of the snout to the root of the tail. Many species display a very interesting courtship behavior. Fishes formerly assigned to the genus *Mollienesia* are now classified as belonging to the genus *Poecilia*, as are those of the former genus *Limia*. Species within the *Mollienesia* and *Limia* group have a tendency toward hybridization. For this reason the aquarist should never maintain different fishes of the *Limia* and *Mollienesia* groups in the same aquarium. The following species also belong to the *Limia* group: *Poecilia vittata, P. ornata, P. caudofasciata, P. domeniciensis,* and *P. versicolor.*

Many *Poecilia* species have found their way into the tanks of hobbyists. During the last few years in particular, many a species regarded as unavailable could once again be imported and purchased by aquarists. Many of the interesting wild forms did not find acceptance within the hobby because their colors are not striking enough, an argument that unfortunately continues to be of prime consideration where the trade is concerned.

Poecilia reticulata—The Guppy

The guppy has been a favorite of hobbyists since 1908. Its status as a premier aquatic pet can hardly be disputed. The fish available on the market today bear little resemblance to the wild forms from Trinidad or Venezuela with their much narrower fins and more subdued colors. The tank-raised strains of the guppy are the products of intraspecific breeding as opposed to the hybridization of the swordtails. That is, varieties of different colors belonging to the same species formed the initial breeding material. Since then more sophisticated guppy cultivation has produced so many fin variations and color varieties that their description alone would fill a book. Today there are regular contests and shows at which the entries are judged according to an international standard of excellence, and many a novice who purchased his first guppies in all innocence remains "hooked" on these

Although the guppies of today are far removed in appearance from the wild-type guppies (contrast the wild type shown above with the highly developed fancy guppies shown below), they are still the same basic fish, with no admixture of other species.

This page and facing page: males of different guppy strains available commercially. Facing page, upper photo: three-quarter blacks; facing page, lower photo: multicolored snakeskins; above, half-black red; below, multicolored delta.

Multicolor snakeskin male guppies

Facing page: female guppies as
well as males also show the
results of selective breeding
over the course of time,
although they don't depart as
much as males do from the
original wild-type guppy stock.

little fish for life.

The guppies most commonly sold by dealers are the deltas, fish with a broad triangular or fan-shaped tail. The purchaser should make sure that the fins are neither retracted nor damaged and that the fish are behaving in a lively manner. Water requirements are a little on the hard side—above 10 DH—rather than soft, and usually the addition of a small quantity of salt would prove helpful. Tank-bred strains require temperatures of between 79° and 82°F. In its native range the guppy is a very adaptable shallow water fish and can be found in a wide variety of habitats including brackish situations. Some aquarists have successfully kept tank-raised strains in strictly saltwater aquariums! Feeding presents no special problems—guppies are omnivorous and will accept a wide variety of dry and live foods. Guppies can be kept in a community tank and adapt very well since they are nonaggressive toward other species. But the hobbyist should remember that the fancy strains will be encumbered by their long flowing finnage and thus the target of the various fin-nipping species. If you have developed a soft spot for the guppy—and almost every aquarist has passed through this phase—maintain a group of these lively but peaceful fish in a good-sized aquarium with plenty of swimming space. Another important hint: isolate the often numerous fry from the parents immediately. Unless the breeding is carefully planned many young may be lost to the often cannibalistic parents.

The untiring male guppy will make seemingly ceaseless mating attempts. Brief contacts are simply "pseudo-copulations," however, with effective union requiring a longer period of time. Once acclimated, one can expect 20 to 60 fry per mature and healthy female at monthly intervals. One problem the hobbyist will sooner or later be confronted with is what to do with all the young? I am not in a position to offer much in the way of concrete advice, but practical alternatives to simply disposing of excess guppies by flushing them

Male guppy displaying before female; the male's colors are at their brightest during the courtship display.

Guppies are relatively very peaceful fish and can be counted on to live at peace with their tankmates—but that doesn't mean that their tankmates are going to live in peace with them. Here a male guppy is being swallowed by a male *Belonesox belizanus*.

down the toilet would be to expand your hobby through more tanks, giving the fry away to interested fellow hobbyists, or perhaps the most sensible of all—keep an oscar or other such guppy-eating fish as an aquatic disposal unit.

Poecilia sphenops—The black molly

It is one of the peculiarities of the Poeciliidae's aquarium history that the wild form of some of the best-known species is unknown to the great majority of aquarists. The well-known black molly is a prime example of this. The wild form of *Poecilia sphenops* lives predominantly in the brackish coastal waters of Venezuela. It is a schooling fish of an unassuming bluish gray coloration with transparent fins, and only the dominant male within the school displays more striking colors. The wild species caused a considerable stir in the scientific world when in southern Mexico a population was discovered living exclusively in caves. In these fish the eyes are reduced in size and there are a number of interesting adaptations to life in a perpetually lightless environment.

The origin of the cultivated black molly is obscure. The black tank-raised strain, which does not occur in nature, probably resulted from consistent inbreeding experiments with different color varieties of the highly mottled *Poecilia sphenops*. As a result of crossing with *Poecilia velifera* and *Poecilia latipinna*, the genetic path of the black molly has turned into a hopelessly convoluted maze, but this has in no way detracted from the popularity of these attractive fish.

The black mollies offered by dealers today consist mostly of Southeast Asian strains with well-developed fins. The species is ideal for the community tank in which the temperature is maintained on the warm side—about 79 °F. In too cold an environment mollies quickly lose their resistance to parasites and become prone to infections of the air bladder. Symptoms of chilling include a fading of the normally vivid jet-black color, swimming lethargically near the substrate, and clustering near the tank's heating unit.

A pair (male in lead) of black mollies, *Poecilia sphenops*.

Lyretailed male black *Poecilia sphenops*.

Feeding is not a problem since the algae that are absolutely essential to their diet can be substituted or supplemented with dried foods containing chlorophyll or by providing crushed or boiled lettuce or spinach leaves.

To provide optimal conditions requires a sunny aquarium with abundant algae and an addition of about 10% salt. However, the fish will do almost equally as well in hard fresh water. At intervals of six to ten weeks about 20 or more fry are produced. If there is adequate plant cover, these will not be molested by the parents. When the fry are several days old their black coloration may fade to gray. There is no cause for alarm, though, for as they grow older the young will turn jet-black like their parents.

Poecilia velifera—The Yucatan sailfin molly

The Yucatan sailfin molly could be aptly described as the flagship among the livebearers. This comparison is inevitable not just because of its stately size (4 to 7 inches) but also because of the magnificent sail-like dorsal fin displayed by the male. Not surprisingly, these fish are the showpiece of many exhibition aquariums, which indicates the nature of the quarters they should be offered. A large aquarium with plenty of swimming space and a few plants in the background will suit the Yucatan sailfin. In its native range—the Yucatan peninsula—this fish occurs predominantly in slightly to strongly brackish waters with a salt content approaching that of pure seawater. Being a very adaptable fish, however, it can just as readily be kept in hard fresh water and, with luck, might even reproduce there. Water temperature should be somewhere between 77 and 82°F. Nowadays it is being bred on a massive scale in Southeast Asian ornamental fish hatcheries.

The courtship behavior of the spectacularly colored males is fascinating to watch. With the strongly patterned sailfin rigidly and broadly displayed, they keep encircling the female. Particularly striking is the broad, vertical mouth

The majestic looks of the Yucatan sailfin molly, *Poecilia velifera*, have made it a sought-after species even though it is not among the easiest of livebearers to care for.

The yellow color in the dorsal fin of the seldom-seen *Poecilia caucana* is distinctive.

Poecilia sphenops pair, mottled variety.

A magnificent *Poecilia petenensis* male photographed during an attempt to capture the attention of a female.

Sailfin mollies exist in albino and xanthistic (golden) forms as well as in variations of the normal wild-type coloration.

with which the fish comb the water surface in search of insects. Dried foods are acceptable in captivity although the species appreciates an occasional feeding of tubifex or white worms. One item the diet must include is algae supplemented by vegetable flakes.

Occasionally larger males will attack smaller fishes, and the hobbyist should bear this in mind when planning the community aquarium. If the fish are kept in pure fresh water, do not raise your breeding hopes too high, as the number of fry likely will not exceed 20 to 40. The real problem, however, lies in raising these slow-growing youngsters. Experience has shown that this succeeds only in spacious tanks with abundant algae and the prudent addition of a tablespoon of salt per gallon. The length of time it takes for the impressive dorsal fin to grow to its full size appears to depend on the capacity of the aquariums. There are reports in which these fins took as little as a year to develop in a 25-gallon tank, though normally full growth takes considerably longer. Good results were also achieved by raising the fish in warm garden ponds overgrown with algae as there does appear to be a connection between a diet rich in natural algae and color intensity. It appears to be likely, though, that the splendid color of the Southeast Asian strains is due partly to the additional administration of hormones!

Dealers often stock specimens of the similar but less spectacular *Poecilia latipinna*, the common sailfin molly of the southern United States, or crosses between *Poecilia velifera* and *Poecilia latipinna*, and the albinistic strains of all these mollies have grown in popularity in recent years. On the whole, the conditions for keeping and breeding these two

Facing page: Some of the fishes of the genus *Poecilia* were placed in different genera until fairly recently. *Poecilia velifera* (male shown in upper photo), for example, was in the genus *Mollienesia*, and *Poecilia melanogaster* (pair shown in lower photo, male below) was in the genus *Limia*.

species are the same, although *Poecilia latipinna* prefers a slightly cooler environment—temperatures from 72° to 77 °F are ideal. Another species displaying a magnificent dorsal fin is *Poecilia petenensis*.

How can these three sailfinned mollies be differentiated? A reliable distinguishing characteristic is the number of rays in the dorsal fin. With practice and patience these can be counted or estimated in the swimming male. *Poecilia latipinna* has 14 rays, while *Poecilia velifera* 18 to 19. In *Poecilia petenensis*, the caudal fin extends into a short sword at the lower edge. These differences apply primarily to the species as imported from the wilds. In tank-bred strains these and other characteristics are likely to overlap since all the species mentioned, including the black molly, often hybridize in the aquarium.

Poecilia melanogaster—
The black-bellied limia, blue limia

This species is one of the most beautiful species of the former genus *Limia*. The fish occurs in the fresh waters of Haiti and Jamaica. They are very lively, extremely agile swimmers, and if kept correctly at 73° to 79 °F and offered plenty of live food will soon display their extremely attractive coloration. The light brown sides shine like deep-blue metal and the tip of the snout and the base of the caudal fin are a rich glowing yellow. The dorsal fin boasts a jet-black pattern, particularly in the male, and the yellow caudal fin has a black margin. Characteristic of the gravid female is a conspicuous black spot. The male bears a black mark on the upper edge of the caudal base. Depending on mood, the fish's sides show fine horizontal stripes and the belly glistens with silver. These fish frequently browse on green algae and should have an aquarium of medium size with plenty of swimming space and abundant plants among which the much-harassed females can hide. The males are fairly ardent suitors and sometimes pursue other Poeciliidae females as well. It is thus perfectly safe to maintain these fish with

Upper photo, male *Poecilia butleri*; lower photo, pair (female above) of *Poecilia melanogaster*.

other energetic livebearers (but no other fishes of the *Limia* group!). The species is rather sensitive to sudden changes in water conditions resulting from major water changes or moving to other quarters but otherwise is no problem to keep. It can also be recommended to beginners who would like to try their hand at a wild form. The female may be gravid for up to eight weeks and then produce between 30 and 50 young. In a densely planted tank no special precautions are necessary. The young, initially grayish in color, grow quickly at first but then, in keeping with most of the *Limia* group, take fairly long to attain sexual maturity and their adult size of 2 3/5 " in males to almost 3 " in females.

Poecilia nigrofasciata—The hump-backed limia

This handsome and interesting livebearer is widely distributed in both fresh and brackish water habitats of Haiti. First imported as early as 1912, these fish have developed into hardy and resistant aquarium stock. The lively but peaceful Poeciliidae of the old genus *Limia* are well-suited for smaller and medium-sized community tanks. Thickly planted aquaria with a temperature of between 77° and 81°F soon induce the fish to show their magnificent deepyellow color. The fish's sides are adorned with seven to eight dark crossbars. The fins are brownish yellow, the dorsal fin standing out with its black speckles. The forehead and anterior portion of the head bear dark "freckles." With increasing age the body of the male begins to develop the rather asymmetrical hump on the back, and combined with a fleshy bulge, the fish looks quite rhombic in shape. Exciting to watch are the antics of courting males. Holding the body horizontally, they move up and down with great ease in front

Facing page, upper photo: pair (male above) of *Poecilia vittata*; lower photo, pair (male below) of *Poecilia nigrofasciata*.

Female *Poecilia vivipara.*

Male *Poecilia mexicana.*

A pair (male is upper fish) of *Alfaro cultratus*, a poeciliid species only rarely available.

Male *Brachyrhaphis holdridgei*.

of the chosen female. At this stage in the courtship countless luminous scales appear on the male's sides. Although these fish are partial to daphnia and other live food, they will not normally molest their relatively large fry. The hobbyist should not expect more than a few young (10 to 30) at each spawning and will have to wait for nearly a year before the sexes show their adult colors and patterns and can be effectively separated. Hump-backed limias become susceptible to disease if their water requirements are not fully met.

Genus *Xiphophorus*—Swordtails and platies

This genus includes what are undoubtedly the most popular livebearers of them all after the guppy: the swordtails and platies. Their range of distribution extends along the east coast of Central America from northern Mexico to northern Honduras. The fish inhabit only pure fresh waters, often the smallest of clear brooks, as well as the shore areas of larger rivers and inland lakes.

Since the range of distribution extends over such an extensive area, it is not surprising that the various species are adapted to vastly differing climatic conditions. A subtropical climate with relatively low nighttime temperatures and a lot of rainfall is present in the north. The countries of Honduras and Guatemala possess a tropical, humid climate. Inevitably, this so ecologically and climatologically varied range of distribution has resulted in an enormous diversity within the genus. This has not only caused considerable taxonomic confusion among scientists but also may form part of the basis for the diversity of form and color among aquarium populations. In some water systems in Mexico platies and swordtails can be seen to co-exist, but hybridization of these closely related species such as occurs in the aquarium has never been observed. Intensive research has shown that in nature any *Xiphophorus* species sharing a restricted space are prevented from interbreeding by a graded system of environmental and behavioral barriers. But even if seasonal flooding

Xiphophorus helleri (male is upper fish in photo above) and *Xiphophorus maculatus* (three males above female in photo below) are the most popular fishes in the genus *Xiphophorus* and have provided colorful, graceful specimens to inhabit hobbyists' tanks for many years.

61

causes the species to intermingle, hybridization is still prevented by reproductive and biological barriers. Due to these facts the genus has become an important research subject. In the swordtails and platies one can still witness the continuing complex process of species formation and differentiation. These studies are, however, possible only in the natural environment of these fishes since the interspecific lines of demarcation are still very faint and sensitive. Varying current speeds within the same body of water, the smallest differences in food and temperature requirements, gradations in the sequence of courtship behavior—these are impossible to duplicate in the home aquarium. Consequently, most of the fishes available on the market today are a mixture of the three basic forms—*Xiphophorus helleri* (the common swordtail) and *Xiphophorus maculatus* and *Xiphophorus variatus* (the platies). The natural division of the *Xiphophorus* species into both populations and subspecies of different colors has resulted in a tremendous color palette that breeders have continued to develop. A common characteristic of the genus is the gonopodium, which, with its distinctive groups of claws and hooks as well as the specialized "thorns" on the lower edge of the third ray, has become the uniting character of the genus. On the other hand, where the females are concerned, external differences between the species can be very difficult to detect. For this reason, the differences in the finer structure of the gonopodium are as important in the determination of species as, for example, the courtship behavior of the males. Characteristic courtship behavior is passed on genetically. Therefore, hybridization can result in its complete loss or reduce it to a virtually functionless level.

Research in the areas of natural species distribution, heredity (genetics), behavior, and morphology (the science of form) have enabled science during the last few decades to draw up a classification based as closely as possible on natural relationships. This was made all the more difficult

Red in its various shades is the color most commonly seen on sword-tails in the hobby; sometimes the red or reddish basic body color suffuses the entire fish, as in the upper fish in the photo above, and sometimes it is combined with other colors, as in the lower individual in the photo above.

by the fact that biologically these fishes did not unconditionally merit description as species. Many aquarists are familiar with the arrangement of the species into three categories (*maculatus*-group, *montezumae*-group, and *helleri*-group) prepared by D. E. Rosen. More recent investigations by C. D. Zander (Zoological Institute of Hamburg University) suggest a much simpler arrangement which appears to be closer to the manner in which these fishes are actually related to one another. This is the division into the platies, species of a rather more robust build without or with only a hint of the sword, and the swordtails, species of a more slender build and generally possessing a distinct sword. According to these investigations, the earlier recognition of subspecies cannot be maintained either since there are too many transitional forms and hence no rigid boundaries.

To the aquarist these results would become important if he were to collect wild specimens and wished to preserve these populations in as pure a form as possible.

The following species are known at the time of this writing. The platy-group, including the "platies" of the aquarium hobby, consists of *Xiphophorus evelynae, X. roseni, X. maculatus, X. variatus, X. milleri, X. couchianus,* and *X. xiphidium*. The "true" swordtails, in which the lower section of the caudal fin extends into the well-known sword, includes *Xiphophorus helleri, X. pygmaeus, X. montezumae, X. cortezi, X. nigrensis, X. kosszanderi, X. andersi,* and *X. clemenciae*. For the aquarist who has no opportunity to collect the rare and often tricky wild forms, there remains the choice of three approved species and their tank-bred strains: *Xiphophorus helleri, X. maculatus,* and *X. variatus.*

Xiphophorus helleri—Swordtail, helleri

Most aquarists have kept the green swordtail or helleri at some time or other. Unfortunately the green "wild form" has been eclipsed in popularity by tank-bred forms of other and brighter colors. Originating in swift-flowing waters, the

Upper photo: male wagtail swordtail. Lower photo: pair (male above) of red swordtails.

green swordtail needs spacious, longer aquaria with clear water. An efficient filtration system is necessary, and the water should be changed at regular intervals and not overloaded with excess food. The swordtail needs cooler water with a temperature of 68° to 75°F. If the water is too warm, signs of physical degeneration and deterioration will begin to appear in the fish. (This applies only to the more northern variety.) The males of this attractive species show a dark red horizontal band on the flanks which has a yellowish line above it. The long sword-like extension is golden yellow with black edges. The dorsal fin shows fine speckles of dark pigment. The southern variety (formerly *Xiphophorus helleri guentheri*) is not quite as slender in build. The dorsal and caudal fins are dominated by spots of red pigment. In addition, this variety tends to have a pattern of black spots on the sides. These fish will thrive at temperatures of around 77°F.

A school of lively green swordtails is an attractive sight, but the hobbyist should remember that the males will often display considerable aggression toward one another. If limited space is available, the tank should be stocked with one male, several strong females, and such fry as are big enough not to be swallowed. On the other hand, if one has a very large aquarium (50 gallons or more) at one's disposal, then the males should outnumber the females. In this way the formation of territories and the constant squabbles between dominant and submissive males are prevented.

The swordtail diet should present no problems—they eat nearly anything, especially live foods. In addition to daphnia, that also includes their own fry. In nature the water current usually ensures the urgently required separation from the parent fish; the young are carried into quiet bays, overgrown shorelines, or small lakes and thus stand a better chance of reaching maturity. The aquarist should provide a densely planted breeding tank or a standard breeding trap made of plastic.

Why should the descendants of the "wild" green swordtail

Cross-breeding with platies over the years has had a tendency to reduce the size of the sword on male swordtails, as can be seen in the males of the pairs shown in these photos.

be so strongly recommended to every aquarist who has the determination to guarantee perfect water conditions? Because there really is no other livebearer that performs such behavioral fireworks as does this species.

Occasionally the hobbyist will observe that some "females" have suddenly apparently changed into "males." In the past this process was interpreted as a "sex change," but that is not the case. It has since been discovered that among green sword-tail males there are early developers and late developers. Whereas in the "early males" the typical sex characteristics (gonopodium and sword) are formed quite early in life, the "late males" may take between one and two years to complete their sexual development. Surpassing the early males in size, the late males more closely resemble females in their external appearance until they attain sexual maturity.

Swordtail varieties

The numerous tank-bred varieties of the swordtail are a tragic reminder of the degenerative processes animal species can be subjected to as a result of human intervention in the form of experimental breeding. Although many tank-raised strains display showy colors, such behavioral remnants as remain are pitiful to behold. It is not my intention to discourage the aquarist from creating his or her own swordtail varieties, but it must be pointed out that the cultivation of color characteristics often goes hand in hand with a loss of natural traits which are not immediately obvious.

The red swordtail variety evolved through careful selective breeding and in behavior, appearance, and living requirements remains closely related to the original green form. Specimens that do not show a red horizontal band, however, are a cross between *Xiphophorus helleri* and *Xiphophorus maculatus*. In such individuals fertility is often severely reduced. The wagtail helleri is one of the more appealing and resistant swordtail strains. Its basic body color is a rich red, the fins and tip of the tail black in color. Dealers fre-

Bright red wagtail swordtails, male above; in this color variety it is hard to find a male with a fully developed sword.

Above, upper photo: green variegated swordtail pair, male below; lower photo: green swordtail male.

Facing page: top: blood red lyretail swordtail male; center: Berlin lyretail swordtail male; bottom: brick red tuxedo swordtail male.

71

quently offer varieties with longer, veil-like fins. These are infertile as a rule.

Many of the artificially produced swordtail varieties are bred in large hatcheries in Southeast Asia. They are not pure-bred and are marketed solely on the basis of their external appearance. They furthermore tend to be less hardy and thus unusually susceptible to parasitic infestation and bacterial infections. This may well be the result of an excessive and indiscriminate use of hormones and antibiotics in their breeding and rearing. The transition from the warm breeding ponds to tap-water doubtless contributes to their overall fragility. Without exception, all the artificially cultivated varieties require a warmer environment than the wild forms or their pure-bred, tank-raised descendants.

Xiphophorus maculatus—The Platy

The red platy is a fish that can be readily recommended to every novice aquarist. As opposed to the cultivated swordtail varieties, some platy varieties (chief among them the popular red platy) have lost none of their vitality or fertility. These untiringly active, deep-red, peaceful fish are close to ideal community tank tenants and are often kept in decorative association with black mollies. There are many natural color varieties, so the existence of over 40 different varieties and subvarieties produced in captivity should come as no surprise. The red platy favors temperatures of between 72° and 77°F, accepts a wide variety of foods, and can produce 50 or more young at intervals of four to six weeks. If many fry are desired, it would be best to use a separate tank or a spawning trap. In a well-planted tank without predatory fishes there will always be a few survivors among the young. The aquar-

Facing page:
A pair (male above) of red platies; note the over-all solidity of color of these *X. maculatus* as contrasted to the variety of colors on the three male *X. variatus* below.

Above, upper photo: sunset high-fin platy male; lower photo: red tuxedo high-fin platy male.

Facing page, top: gold platy female; center: gold platy male; bottom: pair of gold platies (male leading) exhibiting "Mickey Mouse" pattern.

The successful application of the principles of genetics to fish breeding has resulted in the production of some beautiful new varieties, among them this colorful high-fin variatus platy.

Facing page, top to bottom: Blue high-fin variatus platy male; a pair of sunburst variatus platies, male following; red high-fin variatus platy male.

ist intending to set up a community tank with platies and other livebearers should refrain from adding swordtail varieties to the collection as this would inevitably lead to uncontrolled hybridization. The resulting fry would be guaranteed to give the breeder little pleasure and fishes of small value.

The red wagtail platy is frequently seen in dealers' tanks. Displaying a deep-red body and beautifully contrasting black fins, the strain has been a favorite with beginning hobbyists for many years. In the tuxedo platy the black color extends onto the sides of the body, while in the moon platy the black markings have been reduced to a round black spot at the base of the caudal.

Xiphophorus variatus—The platy variatus

The robust platy variatus or variegated platy can also be recommended to beginners. This species, called the "parrot platy" in German, is almost as colorful in its natural form as in aquarium-raised fish. A red or yellow dorsal fin contrasts with a steel-blue iridescent body. The wild form inhabits the waters of the country around the Mexican cities of Tampico and Veracruz. There it occurs in fast-moving waters, often at higher altitudes, thus the temperatures in the aquarium should not exceed 68° to 75°F. The variegated platy average 1½ inches in length, slightly larger than the red platy. It can be distinguished from the latter by the somewhat more slender body shape, which is more like that of the swordtail.

For breeding briefly raise the temperature to 79°F. It is advisable to supplement the normal diet with vegetable foods. In a larger female, the brood will often number more than 100 fry. A particularly beautiful tank-produced variety is the black variegated platy, in which the yellow head and belly contrast sharply with a lustrous black body ending in a caudal fin of a delicate orange color. It is important not to maintain *Xiphophorus variatus* at too high a temperature at any time of the year. This is the most common cause of breeding and rearing failures.

Black variatus platy males.

Male variatus platies sparring with one another during a not-too-serious squabble over females or territory.

Other *Xiphophorus* species

The species *Xiphophorus montezumae* and *Xiphophorus pygmaeus*, now being imported on occasion, have proven to be difficult to keep. One probable reason for this is the fact that they are true wild species, that is, species which were collected in their natural environment and transported straight into the aquarium. The dwarf swordtail, *Xiphophorus pygmaeus*, is considerably smaller than *Xiphophorus helleri* and needs a large aquarium so it can establish and defend its sizeable individual territories. In addition, this species lives in fast-flowing waters and requires strong water movement in the aquarium environment. Breeding reports for the species are not impressive, and results range from five to a maximum of ten fry.

Strong water movement is also required by the *montezumae* swordtail, which in addition requires cooler water (72° to 75°F) rich in oxygen. Breeding experiments with these and other rarely imported *Xiphophorus* species are still in their earlier stages and should be attempted only by experienced aquarists. Since these fishes are not normally available through retail or wholesale dealers, they can only be obtained through contacts with the specialty societies.

Genus *Belonesox*

Belonesox belizanus—The pike top minnow

This genus contains the largest of the livebearers. Female pike top minnows may attain a length of up to 8 inches, the males about half that size. These fish are true predators and in appearance and dietary habits are every bit as impressive as our native pikes and pickerels. The genus is monotypic; that is, it consists of a single species, the pike top minnow, *Belonesox belizanus*. The species occurs in southern Mexico, the Yucatan peninsula, and in northern Central America. In the wild state these fish prefer all kinds of stagnant, often boggy waters, and that preference almost caused their down-

Male *Xiphophorus clemenciae*.

Male *Xiphophorus cortezi*; now considered to be a full species, *X. cortezi* was until recently thought of as a subspecies of *X. montezumae*.

fall. It is in just those kinds of waters that mosquito larvae also develop and proliferate. As a result of massive extermination campaigns using dangerous pesticides, not only were the vectors of malaria destroyed but this unique predatory fish as well. The species had already been considered extinct when in recent years reports by aquarists visiting the region gave cause for renewed optimism. The pike top minnows available to the hobbyist today are largely the tank-bred descendants of a few past "vacation souvenirs"!

The pike-like predatory fish hold an irresistible fascination for many aquarists. Most hobbyists have at least pondered keeping a pike in the aquarium and watching it devour its living prey, and this desire often proves to be the beginning of the end for many a pike top minnow. Once purchased the fish presents the unsuspecting hobbyist with problems for which there are virtually no solutions. To begin with, where to house the gray-green, black-spotted predator? The community tank is definitely not the right place, although the pike top minnow would certainly find the abundant food supply to its liking. The eventual size reached by this fish rules out the 10-gallon tank as well. Temperature requirements range between 68° and 85°F and therefore are not of primary importance. The addition of a teaspoon of salt per gallon of water neither does any harm nor is it absolutely vital. What is important is that the spacious tank be densely planted and offer a large surface area. The pike top minnow likes to hide in the upper water levels among the vegetation, awaiting passing prey. The much larger females are dominant over the males, and for this reason even a relatively large aquarium should not be stocked with more than one pair or several females of similar size.

In the fading light of the evening hours the coloration of the pike top minnow is at its most beautiful. The otherwise yellowish translucent fins become dark, almost black, as do the sides below the lateral line. The large eyes stand out strikingly with their golden reflections.

The male is the lower fish in both of these photos of *Belonesox beli-zanus*, which show two different color phases of the species.

The fry, numbering around 50 though often less, must be protected from the mother immediately after birth by providing a dense cover of floating plants and effecting early removal from the tank. They can be given their first meal of daphnia as soon as they are born. The young *Belonesox* in my own tanks even accepted the occasional offer of dried food.

Food-fish culture is the magic word in the care and breeding of these difficult livebearers. For many hobbyists an efficient guppy culture program is the most important prerequisite when it comes to offering *Belonesox* the best possible care. The hobbyist may also attempt to culture other hearty live foods such as earthworms, aquatic insects, and brine shrimp.

Genus *Gambusia*

Gambusia, the mosquito fishes, are among the hardiest and therefore biologically most successful of the Poeciliidae. With more than 35 known species, the native range extends from the eastern coast of the United States south to northern Colombia. Some species have been introduced worldwide and can today be collected in the boggy ponds of Spain, Italy, Yugoslavia, the Philippines, New Guinea, and Australia. Biological methods of controlling the malarial mosquitoes, once viewed very favorably, are now under criticism because of their adverse effect on local fauna. In many areas the robust, extremely prolific *Gambusia* have caused a reduction in the numbers of native fishes, such as the Middle Eastern species *Aphanius fasciatus*, or perhaps even brought about their extinction.

Aquarists usually keep *Gambusia affinis* as its requirements are easily satisfied. For short periods the species can tolerate temperatures below 50°F, and water quality is not critical. This fish is somewhat difficult to breed in the aquarium since the fry are usually devoured immediately after birth. In garden ponds, on the other hand, *Gambusia* can be kept and bred quite successfully. Outdoor ponds obviously offer better hiding places and a better nutritional foundation.

Female *Gambusia affinis*; easily confused with a female guppy—at least a wild-type female guppy—the female *Gambusia* is much larger than the male.

A pair (male below) of one of the less plainly colored *Gambusia* species, probably *Gambusia atrora*.

Gambusia are less suited to the community tank as the females in particular can be very aggressive. Ideally, the species should be kept in densely planted aquaria without additional heating. Live food should constitute the bulk of the diet, although flake foods are accepted. Gravid females will produce around 50 young after a gestation period of about six weeks.

Other poeciliid genera

The number of wild livebearer species maintained by professional aquarists today is considerable. Nevertheless, such generic names as *Carlhubbsia, Brachyrhaphis, Phalloceros,* or *Priapichthys* will be familiar only to a minority of hobbyists, and this is likely to remain the case for some time to come. The goal of these specialized aquarists should be to develop further species and new imports by means of breeding experiments and selection so that one day they might be made available to a broader circle of hobbyists.

As opposed to those species discussed earlier, many of the wild species distinguish themselves by a long or even bizarrely extended gonopodium. In fact, this often has an effect on courtship behavior: The males slowly approach a female and briefly, more or less in passing, insert their gonopodium. Unfortunately there are few detailed reports on behavioral observations as yet, another reason for devoting more time to one of these uncommon species.

Girardinus metallicus—The girardinus

These peaceful livebearers occur in flowing streams in Cuba. Given good water circulation and filtration and partial water changes at regular intervals, they are easy to keep and breed at temperatures of between 72° and 77°F.

The green to yellowish gray fish show a strong scale pattern and a light metallic sheen on the sides. The males may be deep black on the throat and abdomen, this color often extending to the middle of the gonopodium. The diet of these

The much smaller male of this pair of *Girardinus metallicus* is approaching the female from the rear and slightly to the side, with gonopodium moved partially forward prior to actual mating contact.

Giradinus metallicus pair, male above.

fish is easy to provide, the species accepting most varieties of dry foods as well as live or frozen foods. The males eventually reach a size of 2 inches, while the females attain a length of 3-3 3/5 inches. Anyone seriously interested in breeding this species should isolate gravid females and separate the fry from the mother as quickly as possible. After 30 to 40 days one can expect about 50 young.

Phallichthys amates—The merry widow

The only particularly striking adornment of this grayish fish is the magnificent dorsal fin with its black margin. Under various circumstances the fin is spread out like a signal flag and makes the very quiet fish appear quite serene. If several individuals are kept in a species tank or with other equally peaceful species in a community tank, the uniformly brown-gray color of the body gradually changes into a dark, bright yellow on the belly and a brown metallic sheen on the back. The net-like scale pattern then becomes very prominent. A strong black vertical line passes along the distal edge of the operculum or gill cover, and another runs through the eye. The fish, which reaches a length of 1 3/5 inches in males and almost 3 inches in females, occurs in smaller stagnant or running bodies of water in Guatemala and a few other regions of Central America. These somewhat shy, quiet fish should be maintained in a school in an aquarium with dense vegetation duplicating as closely as possible the overgrown native waters of the species.

Fish that are not yet fully grown require small live food such as newly hatched daphnia or brine shrimp.

If the fish are kept at 77°F one can expect 10 to 40 fry. These grow very slowly and must be raised on *Artemia*. Sexual maturity is attained at the age of six to eight months.

Another species sometimes kept is *Phallichthys pittieri*. Here both sexes grow slightly larger, 2 2/5 inches in the males and 4 inches in females. Males display six to twelve dark blue vertical bands on the central part of the side.

A pair (male below) of merry widows, *Phallichthys amates*.

The most important differential characteristic by which these two species of *Phallichthys* are separated is their geographical distribution. *Phallichthys amates* lives in the fresh waters of the Atlantic coast of northern Honduras and southern Guatemala. *Phallichthys pittieri* occurs in the waters of eastern Costa Rica and western Panama.

Poeciliopsis gracilis

The genus *Poeciliopsis* has increasingly become the focus of scientific interest in recent years. This is due to the fact that some species of the genus consist solely of females—the so-called Amazonian populations (but not to be confused with the Amazon molly). "True" fertilization is not necessary for the development of the eggs of these Amazons. All that is required is the presence of spermatozoa from a closely related species. This peculiarity of reproductive biology is known as "gynogenesis". The Amazons live in neighborly association with a closely related normal, bisexual species. Through fighting, the males of the bisexual species establish a hierarchy among themselves which permits only the strongest males to mate with the females of their own species. The weaker, submissive males are prevented from mating with the females of their own species but are courted all the more ardently by the Amazonian females. Such a uni-sexual/bisexual complex is formed by the species *Poeciliopsis lucida* and *Poeciliopsis monacha*.

Poeciliopsis gracilis also shows a peculiarity of reproduction—superfetation. This species, which is peaceful and easy to keep, inhabits ponds and drainage ditches in southern Mexico and Guatemala. Beside the females with their length of up to almost 3 inches, the males, measuring a bit over 1 inch at the most, look rather dwarfish. The irregular speckles forming a row on each side are sometimes covered with a blue metallic sheen. The species is not demanding in its requirements and can be kept equally well in small aquaria or medium-sized community tanks. The tempera-

A pair (male below) of *Phalloceros caudomaculatus*, black-splotched
color variety.

ture can fluctuate around 77 °F. Over a period of about ten days, two to four fry are dropped daily. No gravid spot of any kind is evident in the highly gravid female to announce the impending event.

Heterandria formosa—The dwarf top minnow, least killifish

Dwarf top minnows are born small, with a length of just a few millimeters. Until the females reach their final adult size of a proud 1 1/5 inches and the males reach their imposing size of 4/5 inches, they require daily generous feedings of brine shrimp and fine powdered food, brine shrimp nauplii predominating. Immediately after birth the minute fry should be offered infusoria since brine shrimp are still too large for them at this stage.

The adult fish swim quietly throughout the tank, stopping at frequent intervals to search the plants for anything edible. Their interesting coloration only becomes apparent when one takes a closer look. The brown ground color is divided horizontally by a black zigzag band. The upper part of the body shows a greenish iridescence and in the male it is adorned with fine vertical striations. The bases of the dorsal and anal fins are marked with heavy brown spots. Dwarf top minnows should not be maintained in too small a container but rather kept in at least a 5-gallon aquarium. They prefer dense vegetation with small clearings at the various water levels. The plants in the tank should be of the delicately feathered type such as *Myriophyllum* or *Cabomba*, and adequate hiding places among the roots are as important as providing *Riccia* or other surface plants. The native range of *Heterandria formosa* extends from South Carolina to Louisiana in the United States. The species occurs in a variety of habitats from overgrown ponds to drainage ditches and bogs, hence wide temperature fluctuations between 59° and 86 °F are tolerated. Heating is thus not required in the home aquarium.

Both of these photos of *Heterandria formosa* shows the great disparity in size between male and female; the fish shown in the trio in the lower photo are younger than those shown above, but the disparity in size is clearly evident in both groups.

If the fish are fed well there will always be a few survivors among the fry, so there should be no cause for concern regarding maintaining a constant aquarium population. In my own tanks, an association with other peaceful livebearers has always resulted in satisfactory breeding and maintenance results.

Priapella intermedia—The blue-eyed livebearer

The genus *Priapella* occurs in the headwaters of streams flowing into the Gulf of Campeche in southeastern Mexico. *Priapella intermedia* was first imported several decades ago, and the descendants of these fish have since been selectively bred into a fixed aquarium strain. Unfortunately these fish are still only rarely available to the general hobbyist, not only because they are very popular among livebearer specialists but also because of the small number of fry they produce in the aquarium. Raising the fry normally does not present any great problem, however. *Priapella intermedia,* in nature as well as in the aquarium, is a highly social creature dependent on the association of the school. As in their natural habitat, the fish require clear, flowing water of around 77 °F with plenty of swimming space in the middle and upper water layers. The species thus should not be kept in aquaria of less than 25 gallons capacity, an added benefit being the full development of their attractive colors under large schooling conditions. The rather translucent body varies between copper and olive-yellow.

Priapella is a surface-feeder and should be offered wingless fruitflies at regular intervals. Where algae are absent it is essential to supply dried food with a vegetable base.

The sexes are easy to differentiate. The females attain a length of up to 2 2/5-2 4/5 inches and with increasing age show a more robust shape without, however, displaying the conspicuous "gravid spot" that can be seen in other livebearing fishes. The males early develop a scale keel on the distal portion of the abdomen and thus can be identified prior to the development of the gonopodium.

Female *Heterandria bimaculata* dropping young.

A pair (male is lower fish) of *Priapella intermedia*.

Family Goodeidae

The Goodeidae is a relatively small family of fishes with a distribution that is entirely confined to the highland plateau region of western Mexico. Goodeids are found mainly in the watershed area of the Rio Lerma at altitudes of between 2800 and 6000 ft. The range of this family is characterized by an absence of primary freshwater fishes, and consequently the Goodeidae was able to diverge into many species and occupy numerous ecological niches. A further characteristic of these fishes is their ability to adapt to abrupt changes in climatic conditions such as often dramatic temperature changes.

Goodeids have been kept in aquaria for only a relatively short time but have proven hardy and adaptable if their undemanding needs are met.

The shape of the body in this group of very active swimmers is determined largely by the particular habitat. What they all have in common, however, is a narrow, often pointed head and a clearly defined caudal peduncle in which the edges are parallel.

Among the 40 or so known species will be found an astonishing diversity of adaptations. There are species that inhabit springs and streams, while others occur in the smallest of pools and ponds. There are algae-eaters (genus *Ilyodon*) and those that extract their food from the water by means of filtration (genus *Goodea*). Others are omnivores (genus *Xenotoca)* or carnivores (genus *Alloophorus*).

So far, taxonomists have not succeeded in completely sorting out the natural relationships of these fishes. The aquarist is made painfully aware of this every time the generic and specific names change, which is often. All the known goodeid species are currently being kept and studied under laboratory conditions, and this research is likely to continue for some time. Earlier taxonomic classifications were based on since disputed variations in the trophotaenia or embryonic feeding tapes, the Goodeidae being viviparous or true

Shown here are two of the less commonly seen goodeid species; above is a male *Ilyodon xantusi*, and below is a male *Ataeniobius toweri*.

97

livebearing fishes. This evolutionally advanced state of embryonic nutrition, however, makes it seem strangely contradictory that a proper copulatory organ is absent in goodeid males. The only notable adaptation visible in the latter's anal fin is the bending downward of the first six or seven rays to form a short "flap" entirely separate from the rest of the fin. It was not until comparatively recently that close observation of *Goodea atripinnis* revealed that the male anal fin was not in fact a modified gonopodium as suggested in the literature.

For copulation to succeed, it is essential that both fish synchronize both sexual readiness and movements. The male presses himself closely against the female and forces a muscular, tube-like extension of his genital pore against that of the female. To ensure that the sperm, which is not transmitted in parcel form, reaches its destination the male then places the flap around the two genital pores rather in the manner of a folded hand. In this way a pocket is formed which effectively aids in the transmission of the sperm. It has since been suggested by ichthyologists Miller and Fitzsimons that the term "gonopodium" not be applied to the goodeid anal fin.

Xenotoca eiseni—The orange-tailed goodeid

Within the few years of its introduction to aquaria this species has developed into a full-fledged aquarium fish. It is not difficult to propagate and is highly prolific, easy to keep, and of attractive coloration. In short, it possesses all the attributes a livebearer should have if it is to gain real popularity among hobbyists.

The body of fully grown males is almost circular in cross-section and the narrow, pointed head has rather small eyes.

Facing page: The upper photo shows a *Xenotoca eiseni* pair mating; the lower photo shows a very heavily pregnant female *X. eiseni*, with the eye of a fry very clearly visible through the skin of the mother.

The comparatively narrow, pigmented caudal peduncle contrasts strikingly with the rather robust body. The anterior part of the body is adorned with a band of metallic pale blue while the posterior part has a bright orange band. The caudal fin of both sexes is of a delicate yellow-orange color. Apart from the population just described, there is another that has also been imported. This is slightly more slender and shows a hint of vertical banding on the flanks.

These fish are quiet but persistent swimmers that will feel as equally at home in densely planted aquaria as they will in spacious community tanks. They are omnivores with an equal preference for dried and live food but will feed exclusively on algae if no other food is provided for several days.

Xenotoca eiseni, possibly in common with all other Goodeidae, is unable to store sperm. This means that after each birth mating is again required. After about two weeks the growing embryos will be visible through the abdominal wall as dark shapes, and after another two to three weeks birth occurs. The size of the brood varies between 20 and 60 comparatively large fry that under most circumstances are not eaten by the parents. About three months later the young also become sexually mature, so that existing stocks should be culled and sorted after six months.

The growing fry are uniformly olivaceous in color at first and pigmented with dark speckles. It is not until they are about six weeks old that the caudal peduncles of the young males begin to turn orange. At this stage the sexes should be separated to prevent too early a fertilization of the young females, and it is advisable to let the fish grow for a few months before using them for breeding purposes.

Xenotoca variata

This species is doubtless the most handsome goodeid imported so far but still presents considerable difficulties with regard to captive breeding. When measuring about 3 inches the fish are apparently fully grown and in shape resemble

Female *Xenotoca eiseni* in the act of delivering one of the compara-tively very large fry characteristic of this species and many other goodeids.

Ameca splendens. In males the upper half of the sides is dark in color and sprinkled with iridescent golden scales. The anal region is yellowish.

To date there have only been isolated reports of successful breeding. This fact could have a nutritional basis since the goodeids include several species with highly specialized food requirements. Whether other factors such as water chemistry and temperature also play a part is not yet known. Descriptions and analyses of the biotope of *Xenotoca variata* are as yet virtually non-existent.

Ameca splendens—The butterfly goodeid

This is an extremely beautiful species, although initially rather shy. The specimens in my own tanks were about 2½ inches in length, though it is possible that larger sizes are attained in nature.

Particularly during courtship, part of which can only be described as a wild pursuit, the male displays a prominent black horizontal band that traverses the middle of the silvery gray side and extends from the operculum to the caudal peduncle. The upper half of the body displays numerous bright golden scales which glisten beautifully in favorable light. The most striking characteristic of the male, however, is the two deep black and lemon-yellow bars on the distal portion of the caudal fin. The females show a different coloration. The grayish silver body is covered with countless black speckles increasing in density in the abdominal region. Depending on the light, the distal segment of the body has a reddish sheen which is reminiscent of mother-of-pearl.

The species does best in tanks providing abundant plant cover and rockwork and maintained at about 75 °F. Feeding may present problems as dried foods as well as water fleas are accepted only reluctantly or if the fish are very hungry. I have obtained the best results with ample feedings of mosquito larvae and tubifex worms, although with the former care must be taken to prevent the escape of adult mosquitoes!

102

Both photos show pairs of *Ameca splendens*; in each photo the male bears the yellowish band on the tail and has a full lateral stripe.

After six weeks the female gives birth to 10 to 15 fairly large young with a length of about ½ inch. Non-gravid females appear quite sunken in the abdominal region. In this species, as opposed to *Xenotoca eiseni*, the developing embryos cannot be seen through the body wall. The fry are not molested by their parents and are easy to raise. Unlike their parents, the fry in my own aquarium were not overly choosy when it came to food. They were very partial to newly hatched brine shrimp and even attacked daphnia and mosquito larvae that were far too big for them. Nevertheless, the young grow slowly and sex differences do not appear until they are about two months old. At that stage the dorsal and anal fins in the still-speckled young males begin to darken.

In nearly all respects, these peaceful fish are an asset to the community tank.

Xenoophorus captivus

This active, agile species seems to be constantly on the move, this behavior being most apparent in the metallic green males. When not actively driving a female or dancing around her in a courtship display, pursuing tankmates and chasing off rivals, they are industriously plucking algae from the leaves of plants. In keeping with that restless way of life, the fins of the males usually appear rather battered, the pale yellow band on the caudal fin only rarely seen undamaged. Nevertheless, they are suitable for any community tank that has not been reserved for more passive or peaceful species.

Xenoophorus captivus accepts both live and dried foods, but part of its diet must consist of vegetable matter. The latter the fish normally finds for itself in the aquarium, removing algal growth from the plants without nibbling at the leaves themselves. Under such favorable conditions individuals quickly grow to a length of 2-3 inches, the males remaining smaller than the females. The size of broods fluctuates between 10 and 20 fry, and the young are not regarded as prey by their parents.

Xenoophorus captivus pair; the male is the lower fish.

This species requires well-aerated water and, while tolerating temperatures of below 68 °F for short periods since their native waters lie at high altitudes, the average aquarium temperature should not exceed 75 °F. All in all, this delightful fish is one member of the Goodeidae that presents no special problems to the hobbyist.

Family Hemiramphidae— *Halfbeaks*

Geographically speaking, the livebearing halfbeaks of Southeast Asia are the equivalents of the American Poeciliidae. With their characteristic shape they are virtually unmistakable: the lower jaw has evolved into a rigid, often needle-sharp extension while the upper jaw forms a movable, triangular little flap. Just beyond the upper jaw, which is equipped with numerous fine teeth, two finger-like protrusions can be observed on close inspection. These are the nasal tubes holding the highly sensitive olfactory cells. The elongated body bears the dorsal and anal fins in the posterior quarter, giving the halfbeaks a pike-like appearance. To a greater or lesser extent, all of the live-bearing halfbeaks are surface fishes which populate rivers, brooks, and ponds in dense schools and frequent brackish coastal waters as well. A few species also occur in swift streams at relatively high altitudes.

In densely populated areas such as the island of Java, some halfbeak species have become extinct or are extremely fragmented in distribution. This is largely due to the heavy and indiscriminate use of insecticides, and it is probable that in some areas the guppies and *Gambusia* that were introduced into the Indo-Malayan region for the control of the malaria mosquitoes have also contributed to the sharp decline of the halfbeaks.

Here and on a following page are presented photos of the sequence of birth of fry in a hemirhamphid species, *Nomorhamphus liemi*. In the upper photo a fry is emerging head first from the mother; in the lower photo another baby is being delivered tail first.

Few people realize that there also exist normal egg-laying halfbeaks along with livebearing species and that where this family is concerned livebearing is the exception rather than the rule. The classification of the livebearing halfbeaks is not overly complicated, since there are only three common genera, with slightly more than ten recognized species. (There are of course many more egg-laying genera in marine waters.) Representatives of all three genera are occasionally imported as aquarium fishes.

Male halfbeaks are endowed with a well-developed copulatory organ. This, however, possesses the dual function of serving as a locomotory fin and deviates so markedly in its structure that it is not called a gonopodium but an andropodium. In the genera *Dermogenys* and *Nomorhamphus* the shape of the andropodium is very similar.

The posterior segment is similar to the construction of a normal fin as only the first four rays have been transformed into a copulatory organ. The second ray is particularly strong and on its tip bears a three-pronged soft structure which probably figures prominently in the passing of the sperm parcels into the female genital pore. The adapted fin rays are capable of far less movement than those of the gonopodium in the Poeciliidae, for which reason mating halfbeaks always have to press against each other with their bodies positioned sideways. The first rays of the andropodium are normally retracted into a specialized groove in the body, giving the fin a cut-off look.

In the genus *Hemirhamphodon* the structure of the andropodium is altogether different. Here the anterior section looks like a normal fin while the last five rays have been transformed into a shortened, spade-like organ.

The life histories of the livebearing halfbeaks are still largely unresearched.

The halfbeaks, notably the wrestling halfbeak, *Dermogenys pusillus*, have been known to the aquarium hobby for a long time. So far, however, they have been relegated to the side-

Here one of the relatively large fry is just finishing emerging from the mother; in the photo below the just-born fish has headed for its first trip to the surface.

lines as aquarium oddballs and curiosities in spite of not presenting the aquarist with especially thorny problems. Recently, thanks to new imports, interest in these fishes has shown a marked increase. Successful captive breeding of halfbeaks is beset with pitfalls and problems, and to date it has not been possible to cultivate fixed aquarium strains. The halfbeaks available from dealers are primarily imports of wild-caught fishes with all their susceptibility to stress and disease.

Genus *Nomorhamphus*

Yes, they do exist: halfbeaks without "half a beak." The short-snouted halfbeaks of this genus are confined entirely to the Indonesian island of Sulawesi (also called Celebes). The main characteristic of this genus is the only very slightly extended lower jaw, which in the males usually bears a pronounced fleshy appendage at its tip. With a length of up to 4½ inches, these fish grow considerably larger than other familiar livebearing halfbeaks and are of a more robust build as well. Most species imported inhabit fast-flowing mountain brooks with a high oxygen content. Other *Nomorhamphus* species are found in some of the larger lakes of the central Celebes but have not been imported. Many forms have been imported recently from the southern arm of the curiously shaped Southeast Asian island, which will likely be described as new species or subspecies. However, a definitive taxonomic arrangement of these fishes will become possible only after lengthy and thorough investigations.

Nomorhamphus liemi

This species from the southern arm of the island has only recently been described by Vogt. It differs in a few morphological characteristics from *Nomorhamphus celebensis*, which appears to be confined to Lake Posso in central Celebes. It is therefore highly probable that the fish recently described in aquarium literature as *Dermogenys celebensis* were in fact

Above and below: the male (with the colored fins and much larger
"beak" extension) pursues and displays before the female during
courtship.

Nomorhamphus hageni.

Nomorhamphus celebensis.

Closeup of pair of *Nomorhamphus liemi* showing the comparatively much larger lower jaw of the male.

Nomorhamphus liemi. The specimens available on the market today have so far come exclusively from the brooks in the chalk mountains of Maros.

The ground color in the female is a pale olive-gray. The back of the male is bright olive and the sides may have a reddish hue in the anterior region and appear bluish iridescent near the tail. In courting males the belly is of a luminous lemon-yellow. The snout looks as though it had been sprinkled with red powder, and on the tip of the jaw is a red or black fleshy appendage. Equally colorful are the fins. The deep black dorsal, caudal, and anal fins are irregularly marked by red blotches or patches, as are the pectoral and ventral fins. According to Vogt, specimens of this coloration are assigned to the subspecies *Nomorhamphus liemi snijdersi*, whereas in members of the subspecies *Normorhamphus liemi liemi* all the fins are completely black. Like the other halfbeaks, *Nomorhamphus* feeds mainly on flying insects. The stomachs of wild-living *Nomorhamphus* examined were found to contain principally winged ants along with other insects. The fish hunt for their food in eddies close to the shore. They hang just below the water's surface in loose shoals and disappear into the depths at the slightest hint of danger. The waters inhabited by *Nomorhamphus* fluctuate considerably in chemical composition. Depending on whether it was the rainy season or during a drought, pH values of between 6.5 and 8.5 and a carbonate hardness of between 7 and 11° CH have been recorded in personal studies on location.

From these data important hints on how to keep and care for this attractive halfbeak can be gleaned. Provide as spacious an aquarium as possible (20-gallons or more), hard, frequently changed water rich in oxygen, and temperatures of between 68° and 73°F. The fish will go after anything that moves or is introduced into the tank via the filter outflow and they may seize and eat dry foods driven into the tank in that manner. At times, the fish may also forage in the middle

At least two subspecies of *Nomorhamphus liemi* have been described; the black-finned individual above is considered to be of the subspecies *Nomorhamphus liemi liemi*, whereas the individual in the lower photo is a *Nomorhamphus liemi snijdersi*.

water layers as well. The fish are very shy at first and need caves or root tangles to hide in. As opposed to the other half-beaks discussed here, they should not be kept in too shallow an aquarium.

It sometimes happens that the fish suddenly die without apparent reason. I have observed this on several occasions with freshly imported fish, whereas well acclimated fish have proved very robust and hardy. It is possible that many of the mortalities are due to delayed effects of transport stress or that while awaiting sale the fish are kept too warm or given too monotonous a diet. Breeding difficulties may also have nutritional causes. In their natural environment the fish's staple food is primarily ants, and it is possible that this prey contains substances important to the development of the embryos. The 10 to 20 fry, which are all dropped at one time, vary in size when they are born. The first-born may measure as much as 1 inch, while the ones that appear last may be as small as ¾ inch. Shortly after birth the fry become very active and strive to get out of the reach of the bigger members of their species as fast as they can by hiding among floating plants. For good breeding results it is there-fore necessary to isolate the gravid females. It takes some practice to identify the latter, however, since they show neither a "gravid spot" nor a marked increase in their cir-cumference. The embryos do not develop in a bent position like those of other livebearing fishes but lie inside the ovary with their bodies fully stretched out.

Facing page: upper photo shows a male *Nomorhamphus liemi liemi*; the lower photo shows a pair of *Nomorhamphus liemi snijdersi*, male in foreground.

Dermogenys pusillus—The wrestling halfbeak

This species is perhaps the best-known representative of the genus and since 1905 has been turning up in dealers' tanks time and again. Its range of distribution is very wide. In the north it extends from Rangoon over the entire Malayan peninsula (Thailand, Malaysia, Vietnam) to the larger Indonesian islands of Sumatra, Java, Borneo, and Celebes. The species also occurs in the Philippine Islands. As a result of this quite splintered or "insular" distribution, *Dermogenys pusillus* occurs in populations varying considerably in color.

Use of an outside filter will ensure a desirable mild surface current, as these fish have a natural urge to snatch up any insect prey that moves on the surface of the water. *Dermogenys* are highly voracious, foraging not only at the surface but also seeking food in the middle water layers. For this reason both their own fry and the young of other aquarium tenants are at considerable risk! The hobbyist should supply halfbeaks with regular and generous feedings of mosquito larvae, daphnia, houseflies, and small insects collected in fields and brushy areas. These predatory fish will often accept dried foods, but use of commercially prepared fare should be kept to a minimum, particularly if the hobbyist has ideas of spawning his fishes. Pregnant females are readily identified by their prominent gravid spots and their rather "sausage-shaped" bodies. They should be placed in small separate tanks with dense surface vegetation such as *Riccia* and *Nitella*. Newly imported, strong females will often deliver 10 to 30 fry; these are dropped during the night or in the early morning hours and can be separated from the mother in the morning.

Like the poeciliids, *Dermogenys pusillus* is capable of storing sperm.

Halfbeaks have been bred and cultivated for more than a century in Thailand for one reason only: that they exhibit the instinct to fight as persistently and for as long as possible. Cock-fighting in the drinking glass is a Southeast Asian specialty.

An albino specimen of the halfbeak species *Dermogenys pusillus*.

A pair of *Dermogenys pusillus*; the male is the upper fish.

Genus *Hemirhamphodon*

These halfbeaks are distinguished from *Dermogenys* principally by three readily seen characteristics: the andropodium of the males is not shortened but long-finned and protracted; the dorsal fin is situated anterior to the anal fin; and the appendage on the lower jaw is markedly longer than in *Dermogenys* and is covered to the tip with a row of microscopic teeth. Hence the popular name "toothed halfbeak."

Of the three known species, two, *Hemirhamphodon chrysopunctatus* and *H. pogonognathus*, are of significance in the hobby.

Hemirhamphodon chrysopunctatus

This species was discovered on Borneo only quite recently. Large schools of these magnificently colorful fish populate the extremely acid and soft black water of the southeastern part of the island. These halfbeaks are also reported to occur in harder waters as well. The blackwater form makes one think of the neon tetra. Depending on the light, the sides show a glowing band of golden speckles as well as one or more iridescent red stripes. The "beak" is even longer than in *Hemirhamphodon pogonognathus* and in large specimens is iridescent bluish.

So far, little is known about the keeping and breeding of this truly exotic halfbeak.

Hemirhamphodon pogonognathus

These fish, which are occasionally to be seen in the aquarium fish market, come mainly from tropical Malayan forest brooks in the area surrounding Singapore. The base color of the body is a dull olive-gray. The skin fold on the underside of the beak shines ruby-red, as does a narrow wedge-shaped horizontal band on the sides. The fins, especially in the males, are of a translucent yellow color with orange or opalescent bluish edges. In adult males the long tip of the andropodium may extend as far as the base of the caudal fin.

Male *Hemirhamphodon pogonognathus.*

Female *Hemirhamphodon chrysopunctatus.*

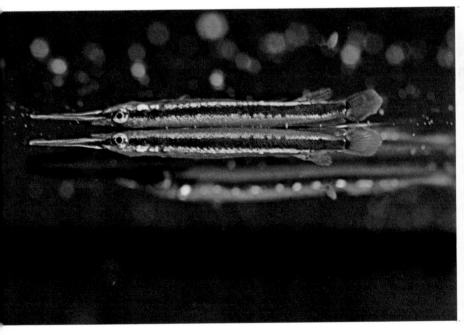

H. pogonognathus makes no impossible demands on its keeper. In water of medium hardness at temperatures of between 75° and 79°F this species does very well. Maintenance and dietary requirements are essentially the same as for *Dermogenys*. Bear in mind, however, that being strictly a surface fish, *H. pogonognathus* only accepts food it finds either on or immediately below the surface.

The fish are much more peaceful than *Dermogenys* and should never be kept in the same aquarium as the latter. *Hemirhamphodon pogonognathus* males, which at 3¾ inches grow markedly larger than the females, tend to squabble among themselves but these altercations can be prevented if one male is quartered with three or four females. Courtship behavior shows less variety than in *Dermogenys pusillus* and does not continue for as long a period.

The fry are not dropped all at once but rather in daily batches of one to three young over a period of several weeks. For breeding, gravid females should be isolated and the fry transferred each morning to a special raising tank with a large surface area.

Family Jenynsiidae

This family was separated from the Poeciliidae because of its different reproductive biology. In addition, these fishes are distinguished by a rather curious characteristic—the females can be fertilized only from the left or from the right side; a projecting scale blocks up the genital opening toward the other side. Interestingly, the gonopodia of the males, too, can move only either to the left or to the right so that a "right" male is able to copulate only with a "left" female and vice-versa.

These fishes are widely distributed in South America south of the Amazon, in Paraguay, Uruguay, and in Argen-

A pair (male is upper fish) of *Jenynsia lineata*.

Anableps anableps cruising at the water's surface in a shallow tank.

tina. Only one species has attained any degree of significance in the aquarium hobby, however.

Jenynsia lineata—The one-sided livebearer

One-sided livebearers appear only rarely in dealers' tanks, yet they are easy to keep and care for.

The pale grayish green fish display stripes of fine spots on the sides and spots of dark pigment in the dorsal and caudal fins. According to the results of on-site studies near Rio de Janeiro, one can distinguish between two types of biotopes. The first consists of fresh- and brackish-water pools, ponds, or lakes as well as drainage canals close to the coast. Further inland the species was found not to occur. The second habitat of *Jenynsia* is characterized by extremely high salinity. East of Rio one-sided livebearers were collected in lagoons which turned out to have three times the salinity of the open sea. Hence the species proves to be extremely adaptable to say the least.

However, while the composition of the water is of no real consequence—*Jenynsia* can be kept in any tap-water of medium hardness—the fish do require plenty of oxygen. Critical points are speedy transporting and careful acclimation. Once the journey has been survived, however, the fish are very resistant to disease in the aquarium. At 77 °F and a mild water current they accept whatever food they are given. The fish are slender, and even gravid females do not become as well-rounded as many Poeciliidae. More than ten young are often produced by younger females. Kept in too small a tank, the fry may be prone to stunted growth. In their natural habitat males attain a maximum size of 1¾ inches while females reach 4¾ inches. If several fish are kept in one aquarium—which because of the right/left-dependency of the sexes is highly advisable—then large females tend to be aggressive toward fishes of their own and of other species. For this reason these fish are not suitable for the community tank, which does limit the number of hobbyists who might

Views (side view above, head-on view below) of the eyes of *Anableps*
as they break through the surface of the water. In the upper photo the
horizontal division of the eye is visible but distorted because of the
surface meniscus.

attempt to maintain them. Nevertheless, anyone with an empty tank should make an attempt at some point to keep this interesting livebearer should the opportunity arise. Much about these fish and their behavior is still unresearched, and observations made by hobbyists are an important source of knowledge and data.

Family Anablepidae

Genus Anableps

These fishes are highly specialized surface-feeders with frog-like protruding eyes. The pupils of their eyes are divided in half horizontally. When *Anableps* swims just below the water's surface the upper pupils are above the water and with the "lower" eyes the fish is able to observe simultaneously what is happening under water. This division of the eyes into two pairs is unique among vertebrates even though, strictly speaking, these "four-eyed" fishes only have two eyes with a total of four pupils. A further characteristic of this family, represented by a single genus, *Anableps*, is the right/ left fertilization technique, shared with *Jenynsia*. The following information was supplied by the staff of the Wilhelma Zoo in Stuttgart, where *Anableps*, once considered a problem species, has been successfully bred since 1972.

Anableps species inhabit the brackish waters of tropical America. The species should be provided with as large an aquarium as possible. The background tank area can be decorated with a strip of "land" providing access to a dry habitat. An efficient external filter is essential, although it will still be necessary to replace one-third of the water each week. For proven best results in both keeping and breeding *Anableps*, the fish should be kept in sea water with a density of 1.007 to 1.011 at 77 °F. The diet should consist of dried

With the fish fully submerged, the division of the eyes of *Anableps* into separate halves is observed.

View from above of an *Anableps* species. *Anableps* often leave the water entirely and actually capture prey (usually small insects) on land.

and living mosquito larvae, crickets, grasshoppers, houseflies, water fleas, mussels, and a variety of dried foods. According to my own experience, these fishes quickly grow tame and literally eat out of one's hand. The size of the broods increases from an initial three to five to 20 fry. They should be raised in shallow tanks on plenty of insects.

A number of *Anableps* species are known, but they all grow to a length of about 12 inches and it takes considerable familiarity with the group to tell them apart. Although somewhat better known to hobbyists today than in the past, the fishes of this genus are yet not often seen in dealers' tanks and probably arrive there only by chance.